W9-AGI-304

Investigating
Why Animals Shed Their Skin

Ellen René

PowerKiDS
press.
New York

In loving memory of my cousin, Marilyn Pardo Liroff

Published in 2009 by The Rosen Publishing Group, Inc.
29 East 21st Street, New York, NY 10010

First Edition

Editor: Joanne Randolph
Book Design: Julio Gil
Photo Researcher: Jessica Gerweck

Photo Credits: Cover, back cover (middle center) © Jim Merli/Getty Images; back cover (top center, top right, middle left, bottom left), pp. 5, 6, 9, 10, 18, 21 Shutterstock.com; back cover (middle right) © Fat Chance Productions; p. 13 © Heidi & Hans-Jurgen Koch/Getty Images; p. 14 © Steimer, C./Peter Arnold Inc.; p. 17 © Flip De Nooyer/Foto Natura/Getty Images.

Library of Congress Cataloging-in-Publication Data

René, Ellen.
    Investigating why animals shed their skin / Ellen Rene. — 1st ed.
        p. cm. — (Science detectives)
    Includes index.
    ISBN 978-1-4042-4486-3 (library binding)
    1. Skin—Juvenile literature. I. Title.
    QL941.R46 2008
    591.47—dc22
                                                    2008010039

Manufactured in the United States of America

Contents

Your Epidermis Is Showing!

Did you know your **epidermis** is showing? Do not worry. It is your skin! It is strong and smooth, and it **stretches**. It is thinnest on your eyelids and thickest on your feet. Like your heart, skin is an **organ**. It grows as you grow.

All animals have skin covering their bodies. Without it, they would dry out. Skin also helps keep bad things out of the body. Warm-blooded animals need skin to keep their bodies from getting too hot or cold. Do you think all animals have skin like yours?

If you weigh 50 pounds (23 kg), 8 pounds (4 kg) of that weight is skin.

This turkey has lots of wrinkly, or folded, skin on its neck and head. Feathers come from the skin on its body.

Is All Skin Alike?

Not all skin is alike. Animals without backbones have very different skin from animals with backbones. Skin may look different from one part of an animal's body to another, too. Many things come from skin, such as hair, nails, claws, feathers, scales, and horns.

All animals shed, or get rid of, skin. Some lose skin in pieces. Others lose it all at once. Some shed skin at certain times in their lives. Others never stop. Many animals also shed some of the things that grow from skin. If you wonder why animals shed, you think like a scientist.

Some birds have scaly skin on their legs, smooth skin under their feathers, wrinkly or folded skin on their head and neck, and hard skin over their bill.

How Do Spiders and Insects Grow?

Spiders and **insects** do not have backbones. Their skin is like a hard shell that keeps them safe and gives them shape. It is called an **exoskeleton**. It does not get bigger when the animal does. How do spiders and insects grow then? They must molt, or shed their skin. Before they do, they make new skin underneath their hard shells. It is folded and squished inside.

When spiders and insects molt, their old shell splits, or breaks open. They wiggle out wearing soft, wrinkly, new skin. Soon the new skin hardens. With each molt, they get bigger.

It might look like this green bug is climbing on a smaller brown bug. The brown bug is really the green bug's old skin!

This frog sits in the water of the pond where it makes its home. A frog's skin is wet even when it is out of the water.

A Yummy Snack

Frogs drink and breathe through their skin. They have mouths, but they do not swallow water like you do. They have lungs, but they need extra **oxygen**. Frogs get it through their skin, mainly when they are underwater. If a frog's skin dries out, it will die. Special parts in frog skin make **mucus** to keep it wet.

Many frogs shed their skin weekly. They twist, turn, bend, and stretch to loosen old skin. Then they pull it off and eat it. Frogs get water and nutrients from their old skin.

If princesses in stories knew more about frogs, they would not kiss them. Many frogs make **poison** in their skin. Poisons protect frogs from their enemies. They make a bad choice for lunch!

All at Once

Snake scales are folds of skin. Between tough scales, skin is thinner and stretchier. When snakes eat a big meal, their skin unfolds. Their bodies get wider. As young snakes grow longer, though, their skin does not grow with them. They need to make larger skin. It is just like when you get new shoes when your feet cannot fit into the old ones.

Snakes shed their skin in one piece. It splits on their heads. To help, they rub their heads against something hard. Then they move between objects that trap and hold the skin. As they slide away, they leave their old skin behind.

Before snakes lose their old skin, they grow new skin underneath. A milky liquid fills the space between the two skins and helps them come apart. This clouds the snake's eyes, which puts it in danger from enemies. Shedding helps the snake, too, though. It gets rid of worn-out scales and bugs on the snake's skin.

Young snakes must shed to grow. Even the snake's eye has skin over it that must be shed.

This turtle's shell is starting to shed. You can see the top part of one of the plates lifting up.

Other Scaly Shedders

Not all **reptiles** shed like snakes. Lizards lose their skin in patches. Their skin may look torn up for a few days. The shedding generally starts with a split on the animal's back. The lizard's new skin is already waiting underneath.

Turtles shed their skin, too. It flakes off their head, neck, and legs. Most turtles have a hard, bony shell that is covered by hard plates. Some turtles, like the common painted turtle, shed the top layer, or part, of these plates. When the common painted turtle finishes shedding, the colors on its shell are brighter.

Do Birds Shed?

Some birds, such as geese, fly south for the winter. They do not want to be molting their wing feathers when it is time to take off for warmer places. Some birds shed once they reach their winter resting places. Others molt after mating. Still others molt at both of these times.

Do you wonder if birds shed their skin? The answer is yes. Bird skin is thin and stretchy. Birds fit loosely inside their skin. It gives them freedom to move during flight. Birds shed skin all the time. It helps get rid of bugs.

Feathers grow from birds' skin. They set birds apart from all other animals. At certain times throughout their lives, birds molt. It replaces worn-out and broken feathers with new ones. Molting birds cannot fly or swim the way they normally do.

These young penguins are shedding their baby feathers. Most penguins get their adult feathers by the time they are two years old.

This deer is shedding the velvet on its antlers. Later the antlers will shed, too. Next year the antlers will grow bigger than the year before.

Oh, Deer!

Mammals with split hooves have horns. Like feathers and hair, horns come from skin. Cattle, antelope, sheep, goats, and other horned animals shed skin and hair. They keep their horns, which grow throughout their lives.

Other hoofed mammals, such as male deer, elks, and moose, have **antlers**. Antlers grow from bony nubs on their heads. Antlers are covered with fuzzy skin called velvet. Once the antlers stop growing, the velvet is shed. Males use antlers to get and fight for **mates**. After the breeding season, males shed their antlers. They will grow new ones next year.

Furry Friends

If you have a dog or cat, then you already know they shed. In fact, they shed a lot! You can see their hair all over the place. Hair comes from skin. It is one of the things that sets mammals, such as dogs, cats, deer, and people, apart from other animals. Hair helps keep mammals warm.

Mammals shed skin, too. The dead skin that flakes off of your furry pet is called dander. Dander does not bother some people, but it makes other people sick. You cannot stop your pets from shedding. It is a natural part of life.

Brushing a long-haired dog helps keep its shedding under control. It also helps keep your pet happy and healthy.

A New You

Animals leave bits of themselves all over the place. Some shed to grow. Other shed to renew skin or replace worn-out skin parts.

You shed, too. In fact, you shed about 9 pounds (4 kg) of skin a year! Every minute about 30,000 to 40,000 dead skin cells flake off your body. They fall on your clothes, bed, desk, and floor. You also lose about 50 to 100 hairs each day.

Do not worry, though. Your body makes hair and skin all the time. In fact, you replace all your skin about every month. Talk about a new you!

Glossary

antlers (ANT-lerz) Large branchlike horns that grow on the heads of some animals and are shed each year.

epidermis (EH-puh-der-mis) The outer layer, or thickness, of skin.

exoskeleton (ek-soh-SKEH-leh-tun) The hard covering on the outside of an animal's body that holds and guards the soft insides.

insects (IN-sekts) Small animals that often have six legs and wings.

mammals (MA-mulz) Warm-blooded animals that have backbones and hair, breathe air, and feed milk to their young.

mates (MAYTS) Male and female animals that come together to make babies.

mucus (MYOO-kus) A thick, slimy liquid produced by the bodies of many animals.

organ (OR-gen) A part inside the body that does a job.

oxygen (OK-sih-jen) A gas that has no color, taste, or odor and is necessary for people and animals to breathe.

reptiles (REP-tylz) Cold-blooded animals with lungs and scales.

stretches (STRECH-ez) Grows bigger when pulled.

Index

A
antlers, 19

B
backbones, 7-8
bodies, 4, 7, 22

C
claws, 7

E
epidermis, 4
exoskeleton, 8
eyelids, 4

F
feathers, 7, 16
feet, 4
frogs, 11

H
hair, 7, 19-20, 22
horns, 7, 19

L
lives, 7, 16, 19-20

M
mammals, 19-20

mucus, 11

N
nails, 7

O
organ, 4

R
reptiles, 15

S
scales, 7, 12
shell(s), 8, 15

Web Sites

Due to the changing nature of Internet links, PowerKids Press has developed an online list of Web sites related to the subject of this book. This site is updated regularly. Please use this link to access the list:
www.powerkidslinks.com/scidet/shed/